DINOSAURS: 101 SUPER FUN FACTS AND AMAZING PICTURES

(FEATURING THE WORLD's TOP 16 DINOSAURS)

Table of Contents

Introduction to the Mysterious World of Dinosaurs

Figure 1: Dinosaurs came in various sizes. They also lived differently. And they often did not get along with each other.

Can you imagine what life would be like if dinosaurs still lived today? Dinosaurs have long been gone, about 65 million years ago. But that does not stop people from finding facts about them. Indeed, they are one of the most interesting creatures that ever roamed the earth.

1. The dinosaur's name came from a Greek word which literally means "terrible lizard." This name is meant to refer to the impressive size of these creatures rather than their scary appearance.

2. Dinosaurs dominated the Earth for more than 160 million years. Sadly, they had become extinct and scientists

believed that a huge asteroid impact or a huge volcanic activity may have been responsible for their extinction.

Figure 2: Some dinosaurs were enormous in sizes while some were rather small like the size of a chicken.

3. Dinosaurs varied in size. The tallest dinosaur can hover above two double decker buses, the heaviest one is about the weight of 17 African elephants, while the smallest is just about the size of a chicken.

4. Most of them may have been massive in size. But they only had tiny brains. The smartest of the bunch would only qualify as a D student.

5. Dinosaurs had different tastes. While some eat all meat, others liked to feed on plants better. In fact, the biggest dinosaurs were herbivores.

Chapter 1: Allosaurus

Figure 3: The allosaurus was one of the huge dinosaurs that fed on other enormous dinosaurs.

The Allosaurus was one of the biggest predators that lived in the late Jurassic period or roughly 150 million years ago. The name means "different lizard."

6. This dinosaur was massive. It stood about 28 feet tall and weighed an average of 2.3 tons.

   Its huge head measured about 3 feet. And it also had a long and heavy tail which made it easier for the Allosaurus to find its balance.

7. The Allosaurus went after the giant sauropod dinosaurs for food.

Figure 4: The allosaurus shared similar features with the T-rex. Like the T-rex, it also walked on two legs and had shorter arms with sharp claws.

8. They looked much like another famous dinosaur, the T-rex. The Allosaurus also walked on two legs, had short arms with three fingers. They have curved claws that were dangerously sharp.

9. These dinosaurs' teeth constantly grew, fell off and replaced by a new set of teeth. Each tooth was at least 3 inches in length.

10. Most of their fossils were retrieved from the Midwest.

11.   The Allosaurus was the first dinosaur to become a movie star in the 1925 version of The Lost World.

Chapter 2: Brachiosaurus

Figure 5: The Brachiosaurus was the tallest dinosaur that ever lived. It used its impressively long neck to reach leaves from the tallest tree branches.

The Brachiosaurus belonged to the group of the sauropod dinosaurs. But they had many features that made them different from other sauropods. These dinosaurs are said to have lived in North America.

12.   Brachiosaurus means "arm lizard." They were named as such because of their distinctive feature referring to

the longer legs in front and shorter in the back. They are the only sauropods that were built as such.

13.   They existed in the late Jurassic period which is about 153 to 154 million years ago.

14.   These dinosaurs were the tallest with a length that measures 85 feet. That is about the same height as stacked up two double decker buses on top of one another. They also weighed about 40 tons.

Figure 6: While the Brachiosaurus had one of the longest necks, it had one of the shortest tails.

15.   They had long necks matched by small heads. And their tails were much shorter too compared to other dinosaurs in their group.

16.   The Brachiosaurus resembled a modern day giraffe. And they fed like one too. A Brachiosaurus could eat leaves from trees even at a nine meter height.

17.   It took an estimated average of 440 and 880 pounds of plants a day to keep the Brachiosaurus satisfied.

Chapter 3: Deinonychus

Figure 7: One of the most fearsome features of the Deinonychus was its terrible claws. In fact, its name describes such a feature.

The Deinonychus lived 115 million years ago. And they were among the fiercest predators.

18.   Deinonychus means "terrible claw."

19.   These dinosaurs' large hands came with three claws each. But the terrible claw was located at the back foot. They had this sickle-shaped claw on each hind foot which was perhaps used for killing their prey.

20.   They may be inferior in size with a height of only 3 feet and a length of 11 feet. But their sharp claws and teeth make them excellent hunters of meat.

21.   The Deinonychus had 60 teeth. And they had twice as many teeth on the bottom of their mouth as those on top.

22.   According to studies, the Deinonychus had the same bite force as that of an alligator.

Figure 8: The Deinonychus was probably one of the scariest dinosaurs and its feathers were not enough to make it look adorable.

23.   These dinosaurs had a few feathers which are believed to have been used for insulation. Studies about

the Deinonychus led to the theory that birds may be this dinosaur's descendants.

Chapter 4: Diplodocus

Figure 9: The Diplodocus was the longest dinosaur that ever lived. Its amazingly long neck and equally long whip tail made it look like a suspension bridge.

Nothing can compete with the Diplodocus when it comes to length. Indeed, they are known to be the longest of all dinosaurs that ever existed.

24.　　The Diplodocus belonged to same group of sauropods as the tallest dinosaur.

25. Measured at 90 feet long, the Diplodocus had an unbelievably long neck matched by their long whip tails. Their structure can be likened to a suspension bridge.

26. They had the same feet as elephants do with five toes. But these dinosaurs had a thumb claw on each of their feet. Such claws may have been used for their protection against their predators.

27. Just like the other sauropods, the Diplodocus dinosaurs were herbivores. Their favorite plant foods include conifers. But they also liked seed ferns, horsetails, club mosses and ferns among others.

28. Their blunt teeth which were located in front of the jaws were used for stripping leaves from branches.

29. Their fossils were discovered from the Rocky Mountains of Montana, Colorado, Wyoming and Utah.

Chapter 5: Elasmosaurus

Figure 10: The Elasmosaurus was one of the dinosaurs that dwelled under water. In fact, it was more comfortable living there probably because it had flippers rather than feet.

Now this is a dinosaur that was made to be on water. The Elasmosaurus lived around 65 to 99 million years ago.

30.   These dinosaurs were excellent swimmers. They had four flippers which allowed them to move through water easily.

31.   The Elasmosaurus was enormously heavy at 2 tons which is why it found it very challenging to stand.

32.   They measured at 46 feet. And more than 50 percent of their length comes from the neck. That made their neck around 25 feet long which means it will take four giraffes to match the length of these dinosaurs' necks.

33.   The Elasmosaurus' favorite meal included squid, fish and other sea creatures.

34.   Their incredible eyesight and their impressively long necks allowed them to hide from schools of fish. And they also had strong jaws.

35.   Rather than roam on land, the Elasmosaurus were more comfortable living in the open ocean.

36.   Fossils of the Elasmosaurus have been recovered from Wyoming and other North American areas.

Chapter 6: Kentrosaurus

Figure 11: The Kentrosaurus was a thorned dinosaur. But rather than using its huge and sharp spikes to hurt other dinosaurs, the Kentrosaurus only used it when it is under attack by meat eating dinosaurs.

Known as a slow moving dinosaur, the Kentrosaurus lived in Africa in the late Jurassic period.

37.   The Kentrosaurus was a herbivore dinosaur.

38.   Its name means "pointed lizard" due to its spikes.

39.   It was 16 feet long and carried a 2 ton weight.

40.   While this dinosaur may be a slow mover, it was perfectly capable of protecting itself from predators using is body armor.

41.   The Kentrosaurus' back had two rows of triangular bony plates. And on its rear were pairs of sharp spikes that may have been around 2 feet long. These sharp spikes extend from the lower back to the tip of the Kentrosaurus' tail. Plus, its hips also carried one pair of impressively long spikes.

Chapter 7: Peteinosaurus

Figure 12: The Peteinosaurus was one of the dinosaurs that could fly.

The Peteinosaurus thrived in the late Trissiac Period. That is about 201 to 252 million years ago. They lived in Italy.

42.   The Peteinosaurus lived to fly.

43.   They had extra long fingers which served to support their rather delicate wing membranes.

44.   The Peteinosaurus liked to eat dragonflies.

45.   Their jaws were filled with short teeth that were needle sharp.

46.   They were only light but they moved impressively fast which made their attacks deadly to their insect prey.

47.   Sometimes, they would cool themselves in the water. And when they did, they constantly checked for land walking predators.

Chapter 8: Plateosaurus

Figure 13: These enormous dinosaurs did not live to prey on animals or their fellow dinosaurs. They were actually vegetarians.

The Plateosaurus is another herbivore that is quite massive in size. It is 27.5 feet long with a weight of 1,500 pounds.

48.   The Plateosaurus had a long neck and tail. Its small head came with a long snout. Its hands had five fingers. This dinosaur also had a large thumb claw. Its other fingers also had smaller claws.

49.   Aside from walking, this dinosaur was also able to use its hands for grasping.

50.   The Plateosaurus' hind legs were much bigger than those in its front.

51.   This dinosaur lived in the late Trissiac period in Europe.

52.   The Europe 219 to 222 million years ago in which the Plateosaurus lived was a dry and desert like environment.

53.   The Plateosaurus was a plant eater. It fed on cycads and conifers. But it swalloned small stones to which helped in digest the tough leaves it ate. The stones helped with grinding the food in the Plateosaurus' stomach.

Figure 14: The Plateosaurus was enormous in size but it was not one of the most intelligent dinosaurs.

54.   While it may have been a huge dinosaur, the Plateosaurus ranked the lowest when it comes to intelligence among the dinosaurs.

55.   Its body and abilities were not enough to defend itself against the meat eaters. The best it could do was outrun its predators.

Chapter 9: Pteranodon

Figure 15: The Pteranodon had been classified as a flying reptile but it was also a close relative of the dinosaurs. This creature had wings but it lacked teeth. Surprisingly, it managed to eat meat, mostly fish.

Rather than a dinosaur, the Pteranodon was actually a flying reptile. It also existed along with dinosaurs and is considered a close relative.

56.   Its name means "winged and toothless." True to its name, the Pteranodon could fly and it literally had no teeth.

57.   The Pteranodon was a meat eater. And it fed on fish most of the time.

58.   It stood 6 feet tall and weighed 55 pounds. It had a wingspan of about 25-33 feet.

59.   The Pteranodon bore a crest on the head and it had a tail that was rather short.

Chapter 10: Stegosaurus

Figure 16: A vegetarian, the Stegosaurus had bony plates on its back and spikes on its tail to protect itself from its predators.

The Stegosaurus was an average sized dinosaur that lived in the late Jurassic period which is about 156 to 140 million years ago. It was about 26 to 30 feet long. And it weighed around 6,800 pounds. It is probably the size of a bus.

60.   Named in 1877, Stegosaurus means "plated lizard" or "roof lizard."

61.   It was a herbivore. This dinosaur particularly liked ferns, cycads, bushy conifers, small club mosses and horsetails.

62.   To protect itself against predators, the Stegosaurus had a total of 17 bony plates. The rows of plates were located on its back. The largest among its triangular plates measured 2.5 feet in both height and length.

63.   In addition to its bony plates, the Stegosaurus also bore spikes at the tip of its tail.

64.   Although this dinosaur is as big as a bus, the Stegosaurus only had a small head. And its brain is only about the size of a walnut.

Chapter 11: Tylosaurus

Figure 17: The Tylosaurus competed with sharks to become a top predator in the ocean.

Existing in the late Cretaceous period or about 80 million years ago, the Tylosaurus weighed 8 tons and was around 15 meters long.

65.   It lived along with sharks; the Tylosaurus was a top predator from the Cretaceous oceans.

66.   The Tylosaurus' favorite food included a variety of fish. It also liked mosasaurs.

Figure 18: These dinosaurs were not fast swimmers so they only preyed on slow moving sea creatures.

67.   It was not a fast swimmer so it liked to hunt for the slow moving prey. But the Tylosaurus also liked to be challenged. So when it felt like it, it would also go after the swift moving prey.

68.   Based on studies, a Tylosaurus could feed on sharks that are 6 meters long.

Chapter 12: Tyrannosaurus

Figure 19: The Tyrannosaurus was a tyrant dinosaur. It was not the tallest, the heaviest, fastest or the most intelligent of all the dinosaurs. But it probably was the meanest of the bunch.

The Tyrannosaurus was probably the most tyrannical dinosaur that ever lived. In fact, its name literally means a "tyrant lizard king."

69. The Tyrannosaurus was a huge dinosaur that had small arms with two fingers.

70. The largest discovered Tyrannosaurus fossils were measured at 42 feet long. But on average, this dinosaur is

about 39 feet long and 20 feet tall. Its weight is just as massive as its height and length at about 7 tons.

71.   This heavyweight dinosaur ruled the dinosaur kingdom 67 to 65 million years ago. They are believed to have lived in Asia and North America.

72.   This meat eater's favorite meal included large dinosaurs such as the Triceratops.

Figure 20: This dinosaur's terrible claws, sharp teeth and strong jaws made it look scary. But what was even scarier about this dinosaur was its keen sense of smell and its incredible speed. It could not only smell its prey from afar, it could also run after them at such an amazing speed.

73. The Tyrannosaurus's cone shaped and serrated teeth were perfect for tearing up meat. Its set of teeth was continuously replaced in case one fell off.

74. It also had massive jaws that carried blade like teeth of about 50 to 60. Its teeth were as long as 9 inches.

75. The Tyrannosaurus always had its tail stretched out so it could balance itself.

76. Despite its weight and size, the Tyrannosaurus was quite capable of running as fast as 20 miles per hour. In fact, one step could make it cover 15 feet.

77. Aside from its sharp teeth, incredible speed, fearsome claws, and massive size, this predator also had an excellent sense of smell.

78. This dinosaur started to become popular when it starred in the Jurassic Park movies. It probably has the most media exposure.

Chapter 13: Triceratops

Figure 21: The Triceratops' three horns were not enough to intimidate other dinosaurs. In fact, the T-rex often bullied and ate the Triceratops.

Aside from being the T-Rex's favorite meal, the Triceratops also had a few notable characteristics.

79.   The name means "three horned face" accounting for this dinosaur's most distinctive feature.

80.   The Triceratops is about 30 feet long and weighed 9.3 tons. When measured at the hips, this dinosaur stood 7 feet tall.

81.   Its favorite food was plants.

82. The Triceratops' skull is simply massive. In fact, a discovered fossil weighed over 3.3 tons.

83. This dinosaur used its horns that could grow as long as 3 feet to charge against its predators the way a rhinoceros would do.

Chapter 14: Velociraptor

Figure 22: This dinosaur was incredibly light at only a hundred pounds. Although it had a stick figure, it was one of the top predators. Named as "swift plunderer," this dinosaur could outrun the bigger ones.

The Velociraptor was smaller compared to other dinosaurs. But it was one of the most dangerous predators 99 to 65 million years ago.

84.   Velociraptor literally means "swift plunderer."

85.   It only weighed 100 pounds and only about six feet long. But it had razor sharp teeth with saw edges made for tearing its prey apart.

86.   Just like the T-rex and other predator dinosaurs, the Velociraptor also had a sickle shaped claw found on the second toe of its hind legs.

87.   Because of its size and weight, this dinosaur could move quickly. It also had excellent eyesight. And compared to other dinosaurs, this one was smart too.

88.   A ferocious killer, the Velociraptor ripped its prey apart and fed on their insides.

89.   Its favorite food was dinosaurs of other kinds, specifically the plant eaters that were slow moving.

90.   The Velociraptor dinosaurs practiced teamwork. They had a habit of travelling and hunting in groups so a kill was almost always a guarantee.

Chapter 15: Spinosaurus

Figure 23: The Spinosaurus was another meat eating dinosaur that had an incredible size. These dinosaurs would eat anything whether it was dead or alive. It would even feast on other dinosaur's eggs.

The Spinosaurus is another powerful eating dinosaur. Its name stands for "thorn lizard." It lived around 144 to 99 million years ago, in the early Cretaceous period.

91.   The Spinosaurus is about 49 feet long and weighed around 4 and a half tons.

92.   This dinosaur lived in Egypt, Tunisia, Morocco and Niger which were only food plains with rich forests then.

93.   It would eat other dinosaurs dead or alive. The Spinosaurus also occasionally ate dinosaur eggs.

Figure 24: This dinosaur had sickle sharp claws, terrifyingly sharp teeth and crocodile jaws. These were enough to keep the vegetarian dinosaurs from running.

94.   The Spinosaurus got its name for the spines on its backbone. These spines were also covered with a layer of skin.

95.   Its jaws were similar to those of a crocodile. And like other meat eating dinosaurs, the Spinosaurus also had a needle sharp set of teeth.

Chapter 16: Archaeopteryx

Figure 25: The Archaeopteryx was the earliest bird that lived. But this was one confused creature. Although it had the features of a common bird, it also shared some characteristics with dinosaurs.

The Archaeopteryx lived around 150 million years ago during the late Jurassic period.

96.   Named the "ancient wing," the Archaeopteryx is the earliest known bird.

97.   It was only a foot long from its beak down to the tip of the tail. The Archaeopteryx's wingspan was only 1.5 feet.

98.   The Archaeopteryx was incredibly light weight at only 11 to 18 ounces. It was only about the size of a crow.

99.   Far from the modern day bird, the Archaeopteryx had three claws located on each of its wings. It had teeth, breastbone, belly ribs and a bony tail.

Figure 26: The Archaeopteryx did not only look a little like a peacock. It also moved like one because it probably did more running than flying because of its delicate wings.

100.   It could fly just fine but it was not capable of flying out too far. This makes the Archaeopteryx much like a peacock that runs more than it flies.

101.   While it may look like a bird, the Archaeopteryx also had characteristics that made it much like dinosaurs such as its horny bill, skull, teeth and other bone structures.

Made in the USA
San Bernardino, CA
09 April 2017